Watercraft

by Tiffany Peterson

illustrations by David Westerfield

Heinemann Library
Chicago, Illinois

© 2003 Heinemann Library
a division of Reed Elsevier Inc.
Chicago, Illinois

Customer Service 888-454-2279
Visit our website at www.heinemannlibrary.com

Designed by Depke Design
Illustrated by David Westerfield
Photograph p.4 by Kimberly Saar
Printed and bound in the United States by Lake Book Manufacturing, Inc.

07 06 05 04 03
10 9 8 7 6 5 4 3 2 1

Library of Congress Cataloging-in-Publication Data
Peterson, Tiffany.
   Watercraft / Tiffany Peterson; illustrations by David Westerfield.
      p. cm. -- (Draw it!)
Summary: Presents instructions for drawing various boats, ship, and other
watercraft, including a jet ski, a tall ship, and a riverboat.
Includes bibliographical references and index.
   ISBN 1-4034-0214-0 (HC), 1-4034-4033-6 (Pbk)
   1. Boats and boating in art--Juvenile literature. 2. Drawing--Technique--
Juvenile literature. [1. Boats and boating in art. 2. Drawing--Technique.]
I. Westerfield, David, 1956- ill. II. Title. III. Series.
   NC825.B6P47 2003
   743'.93872--dc21

                              2002015493

Some words are shown in bold, **like this.** You can
find out what they mean by looking in the glossary.

Contents

Introduction

Would you like to improve the picture that you draw?

Well, you can! In this book, the artist has drawn some of your favorite watercraft. He has used lines and shapes to draw each picture in small, simple steps. Follow these steps and your picture will come together for you, too.

Here is advice from the artist:

- Always draw lightly at first.

- Draw all the shapes and pieces in the right places.

- Pay attention to the spaces between the lines as well as the lines themselves.

- Add details and **shading** to finish your drawing.

- And finally, erase the lines you don't need.

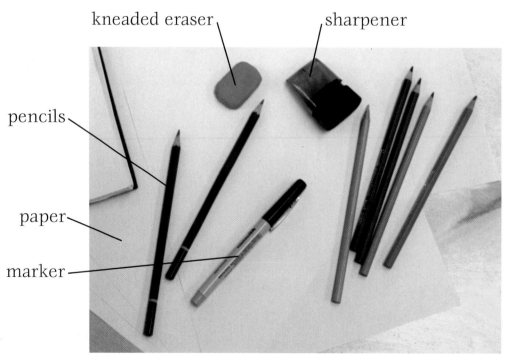

You only need a few supplies to get started.

There are just four things you need for drawing:

- a pencil (medium or soft). You might also use a fine marker or pen to finish your drawing.
- a pencil sharpener.
- paper.
- an eraser. A **kneaded eraser** works best. It can be squeezed into small or odd shapes. This eraser can also make pencil lines lighter without erasing them.

Now, are you ready? Do you have everything?
Then turn the page and let's draw!

The drawings in this book were done by David Westerfield. David started drawing when he was very young. In college, he studied drawing and painting. Now he is a **commercial artist** *who owns his own graphic design business. He has two children, and he likes to draw with them. David's advice to anyone who hopes to become an artist is, "practice, practice, practice—and learn as much as you can from other artists."*

Draw a Los Angeles Class Submarine

Submarines like this have nuclear engines powered by heat instead of by gasoline. Subs can stay under water for long periods. In fact, some travel around the entire world without surfacing, or coming out of the water.

 Sketch a long thin oval, like a hot dog, that is pointed at one end. This is your **guideline.**

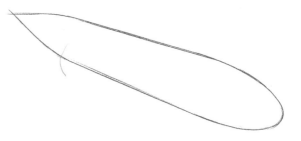

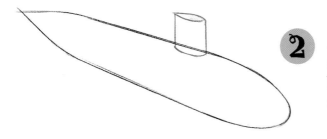

2 Add a square with rounded corners. Draw a curved line between the two top corners to make it look like a tube.

 Add a slanted rectangle for one wing and a shape like a 7 for the other wing that is hidden. Draw four poles, or **antennae.** Add a small rectangle on the top of the tube.

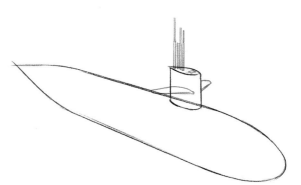

4 Near the oval's point, sketch a triangle with the top point cut off. Add the same kind of triangle, but smaller, pointing down below the point. Near the oval's point, draw two **horizontal** lines attached to a square for a fin. Add a tiny square for the other, mostly hidden fin.

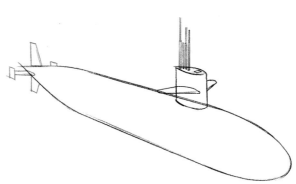

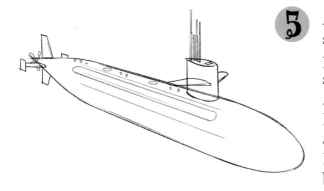

5 Add the **propeller** by drawing two small raindrop shapes at the oval's point. Add details to the top of the submarine. Sketch a long thin oval. Add a parallel line below the oval. Draw three sets of two small dots above the oval. Space them evenly. Draw two circles in the spaces between the sets of dots.

6 Erase the guidelines you no longer need. Darken the details and outline. Draw a line across the middle of the submarine. **Shade** the bottom, the fins at the back, and the wings on top. Add more shading along the sides of the tube. Near the front of the submarine, lightly sketch two curved, **vertical** lines. Write "891" above the wing. Write "891" again in smaller writing at the front of the submarine. Add some light, squiggly lines for the ocean.

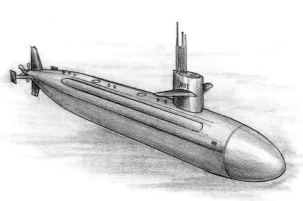

Draw a Sailboat

Sailboats are pushed through water by wind in the sails. This boat is a single **mast** sailboat, which means only one pole holds the sails. The big sail is called the **mainsail.** The smaller one is the **jib.**

1 **Sketch** a pointed oval for the **deck** of the boat.

2 Draw a fingernail shape on the curved end of the deck for the **stern.** Add the **hull** by drawing a curved line from the point of the deck to the bottom of the stern.

3 Sketch a rectangle in the front part of the deck. Draw a slanted line from each top corner of the rectangle to the top **guideline.** On the left side of the rectangle, add a backwards 7 to form another, smaller rectangle. This completes the cabin of the boat. Add two long, **parallel** lines upward at the front of the cabin for the mast.

4 Draw a curved line from the top of the mast for the edge of the mainsail. Draw a **horizontal** line back to the mast for the bottom of the mainsail. Add a dark line along the bottom of the sail for the **boom.** Draw another triangle with two curved sides for the jib.

5 Draw some horizontal lines across the deck to show the floor. Sketch two **vertical** lines on the left rectangle of the cabin for a door. Draw a figure on the stern deck. Add a **rudder** by drawing an upside down L leftward from the figure. Sketch a line from the top of the mainsail to the figure. Draw a curved horizontal line above the deck for a rail on each side. Connect the rail to the deck by drawing some vertical lines.

6 Lightly sketch nine or ten evenly spaced lines from the edge of the mainsail to the mast. Add four darker, shorter lines along the edge of the mainsail. Sketch lines from the corner of each sail for folds. **Shade** the door of the cabin. Add wavy lines for water.

Draw a Junk

Chinese junks can have as many as five **masts** with square sails. The sails are divided by flat pieces of **bamboo.** Sails on junks are lowered or raised by tugging on ropes the way window blinds are lowered or raised in homes.

1 **Sketch** the shape of the **hull.** Start by drawing a shape like a dish. Add the raised **stern,** a rectangular shape on the right side.

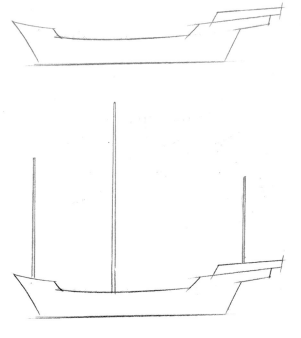

2 Add three **vertical** lines for the masts. There is one mast in the stern, one in the front, and one in the center.

3 Sketch a small tent shape above the stern, a medium tent above the front, and a large one for the center. Curve the right side of the center tent shape.

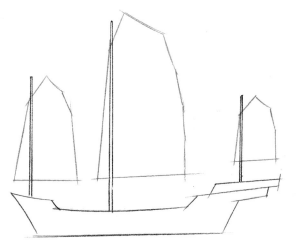

Add **horizontal** and tilted lines across the sails for the bamboo **slats.** The small sail above the stern has three slats. The other sails each have four.

 Draw a long rectangle on top of the stern. Add three posts for railings. Sketch the top of the **rudder** by drawing a jagged hook shape under the stern. Along the middle of the ship, add several uneven squares with vertical lines. These are the railings and posts. Sketch two small overlapping ovals at both the front and back railing for bumpers.

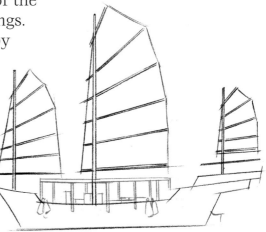

6 Darken the lines of the drawing. Add **shading** across the sails. Draw dark lines across the hull of the ship and short vertical lines on the raised stern. Add wavy lines for water.

Draw an Aircraft Carrier

Military airplanes land on and take off from these huge ships. Because space is limited, a landing plane has a hook that hangs from the back of the plane. The hook catches cables on the **deck** that help the plane stop quickly.

1 **Sketch** a slanted rectangle. At the top of the rectangle, sketch a smaller rectangle with one corner cut off. This shape is the deck of the aircraft carrier.

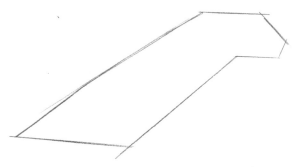

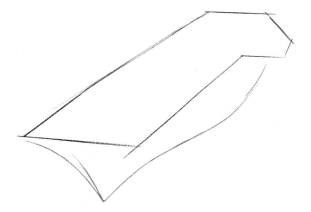

2 Draw a large V under the front of the deck. Connect the V to the back of the deck with a curvy line. Add a curved line inside the V for the front of the **hull.**

3 Draw a small square and a bigger square on top of it. From the right corners of the bigger square, add two small slanted lines. Add a zigzag line upward to the right on top of the upper square. Make the end of the zigzag a slightly long **horizontal** line. Draw a rectangle on top of that line on the left side. Add two **vertical** lines for the **antenna.** From the end of the zigzag's horizontal line, draw a long vertical line. Add a slightly angled line from its end to the small square.

4 Add three horizontal lines to the antenna. Make the lowest lines the longest. Draw two tiny vertical rectangles on it. At the bottom of the antenna, add a circle with a dark dot in the middle for a **radar** dish. Add many vertical lines close together for the tower's windows.

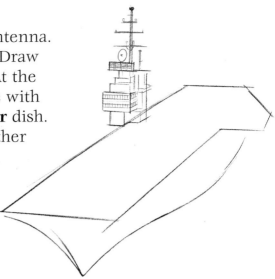

5 Draw a line **parallel** to the side of the main deck. Add a shorter parallel line. Connect them with an angled line to make a small deck. Create a railing by adding parallel lines along the small deck's edge. Draw two sets of two short lines across this deck. Add a short vertical line to create a corner at the back. At the front of the main deck sketch two rectangles. Add several planes on the deck and one coming to land. The fuselages, the bodies of planes, are ovals with pointed tips for noses. Draw triangles for plane wings.

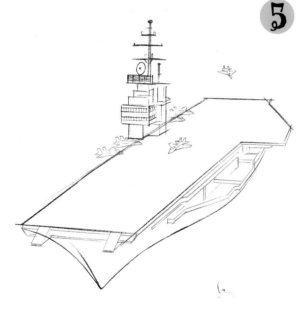

6 Add lines on the deck to show where the planes take off and land. Sketch a shape like an upside down house. Darken the lines of the ship. Add **shading** to the side of the bridge. Shade the hull of the ship and add some dark lines for water.

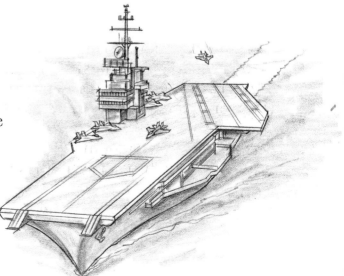

Draw a Jet Ski

The jet ski is a personal watercraft. A driver crouches on the **stern** to drive this small but speedy craft. Jet skis are fun, but drivers must be careful. Because jet skis are so small and fast, accidents can happen more easily than they do with bigger boats.

1 **Sketch** a shape like an arrowhead for a **guideline.**

2 Under the top line add a shorter, curved **parallel.** This will become the steering bar to the handlebars. Sketch two curved lines like skis from the back of the jet ski to the middle to make the top of the **hull.** Extend the upper of these two lines slightly. Extend the lower of these two lines to the front of the jet ski.

3 Draw a long line through the middle of the steering bar to make it boxlike. Add three short lines across the steering bar's right end. Add an oval at the left end. Draw a rectangle for the right handlebar. Draw a curve where the handlebar meets the steering bar. Add a curved line along the bottom for the rest of the hull.

4 Sketch three or four diagonally curved lines from the top of the hull toward the nose to give the hull shape and add decoration. Draw a long line from the bottom of the nose to near the back of the hull. At the back end of that long line, add a nearly **vertical** line to the bottom of the hull. Draw a 7 around the middle where the hull curves up. Draw another 7 on the other side of the hull. Draw lines from the top and bottom of the upper 7 to the back of the hull.

5 Sketch an oval for the body of the driver. Draw a circle for the head. Add an L shape for an arm. Add two more lines for the other arm. Draw curved lines for the driver's hip and thigh. Sketch a leg by drawing two vertical lines.

6 Erase the guidelines you no longer need. Darken the lines. Add **shading** to the top of the jet ski. Shade in the driver's shorts and add a life vest over a T-shirt. Add hair and some sunglasses. Draw wavy and curly lines for water.

Draw a Battleship

A battleship is a large ship **armed** with huge guns. The United States began building battleships in the late 1800s. A total of 85 battleships were built. Some of them are on display around the country.

1 **Sketch** a long thin oval pointed at one end. Draw a short **vertical** line down from the curved part of the oval. Add a long line under the oval. Draw a curvy line upward and connect it to the pointed part of the oval with a **horizontal** line.

2 Draw a line in the shape of four uneven steps from the middle of the boat toward the **stern.** Add a tall rectangle. This is the tower. Draw a long half oval next to the tower. Add two more rectangles as steps.

3 Create box shapes by adding vertical and horizontal lines to the step shapes. Draw a long horizontal box across the tower. Add a horizontal line along the top of the tower. Draw boxes in the middle and the stern.

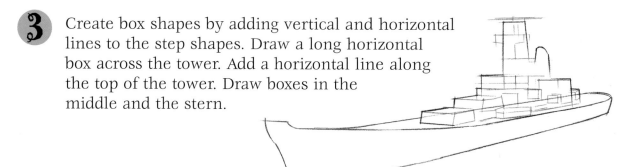

4 Sketch a short, wide rectangle at the **bow.** Add a diagonal and a vertical line in each corner and a plus sign on top. Connect the plus sign's corners with diagonal lines. On the two steps toward the bow, add guns by drawing three squares with long, thin rectangles attached to them. Add other guns toward the stern. Sketch the **radar** tower on top of the long rectangle. Draw a vertical line. Add horizontal lines across it. Draw Xs to connect the lines.

5 Draw short vertical lines along the **hull** of the ship for a railing. Add small circles and squares on and next to the tower for equipment. Draw anchors at the bow by drawing shapes like knotted ropes.

6 Darken the outline of the ship. **Shade** the top of the hull and the front of the tower. Darken the holes for the guns. Write 62 in boxy numbers on the front of the hull. Add some wavy lines along the hull for the water. Add the **horizon** by drawing a wide horizontal line behind the ship.

This drawing is of the HMS *Rose*. The ship was built just like one originally built in 1757 in England. The United States Coast Guard uses the *Rose* as a teaching ship on which people can learn to sail a tall ship.

1 **Sketch** a sideways L and add a curvy **vertical** line from the top. Connect the two lines with a curved line. Add another curved line to finish the **guideline** for the **hull**.

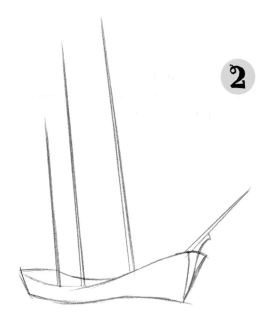

2 Draw two long vertical lines and one shorter one for three **masts**. Draw a very long and skinny triangle coming off the front of the hull for the **bowsprit**. Add a curvy V from the middle of the bowsprit in the center front of the **bow**.

3 Draw two lines from the front mast to the bowsprit. Add two triangular sails. Connect the bottoms of the sails to the **deck** with two lines.

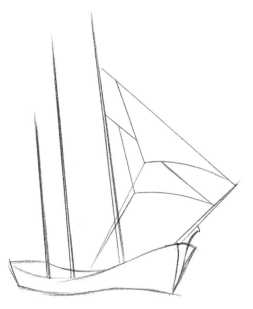

4 Draw four sails on the front mast. For each sail, sketch a rectangle with a curved bottom line. The top sail is the smallest and each one below is bigger than the one above it.

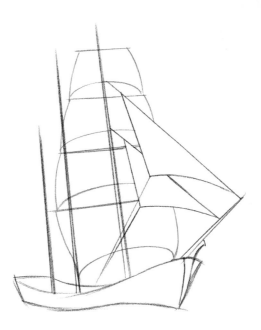

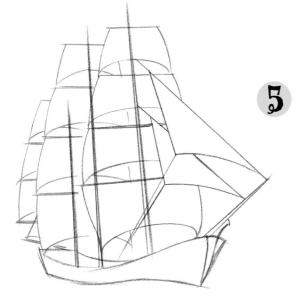

5 Add four sails to the second mast and three to the back mast. A small triangular sail sticks out on the bottom of the third mast. You can sketch the whole sails and then erase the lines hidden by sails in front.

6 Darken all of the lines. Add **crosshatches** for ropes that sailors climb from the deck to the top sails. Add a wavy ribbon on top of each of the two tall masts. **Shade** the corners of the sails. Shade the hull and deck of the ship. Add dark, wavy lines for water.

Draw a Catamaran

Catamarans have two long, narrow **hulls** that are connected. Two hulls make it a good craft for rough water. Catamarans may have sails or motors. They are one of the fastest sailboats, and racing them is a popular sport.

1 Draw two long rectangles with curved ends for the hulls.

2 Connect the hulls with two lines in the middle and four at the back. Near the four lines add a half-moon shape with the top cut off for the **keel.** Add a small half-moon shape for the upper **rudder.** Add an upside down 7 for the lower rudder.

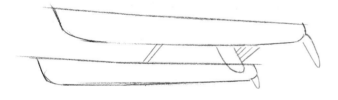

3 **Sketch** the tall **mast.** Add two triangular sails, one on each side of the mast. Slightly curve one side of each sail.

4 Sketch the shape of a sailor by drawing a body, one arm, two legs, and a head. Add a wire from the right sail to the sailor.

5 Add two wires from the top of the mast to the front of the hulls. Draw curved lines across the sails. Add the water line across the lower hull. Draw a line for the **horizon.**

6 Darken the lines of the drawing. Add **shading** in the sails and along the bottoms of the hulls. Write 1016 in boxy letters on the sail. Darken the lines of the sailor. Add shorts and a life vest. Shade the water.

Draw a Hydroplane

Hydroplanes are fast, racing motorboats that look like race cars. When a hydroplane speeds across the water, the **bow** sticks up out of the water.

1 **Sketch** a tube-like shape that gets narrow on one end to become a rounded nose.

2 For the front **hull,** draw a fat oval that has a notch in the back. Draw the back hull as a longer, thinner oval coming to a rounded point.

3 Sketch a slanted rectangle that connects the two hulls. Add a large curved windshield to the body of the boat. Draw a curved line over the back part of the windshield.

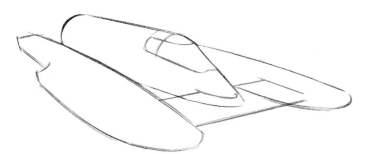

4 Sketch a **spoiler.** Draw two thin curvy rectangles upward from the hulls. Add two **parallel horizontal** lines to connect them. Add pairs of diagonal lines from the rectangles to the back of the hull.

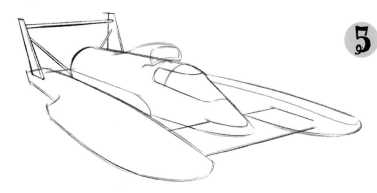

5 On top of the body, add a curved line with a wide oval for the air scoop, which lifts the front out of the water. Add a parallel line above the front hull. Add another parallel line in the back hull.

6 Write Challenger on the side of the body and on top of the front hull. Darken the outline of the boat, the windows, and the air scoop. Add **shading** to the boat. Draw the **horizon** behind the boat and shade the water. Add squiggly lines from the back of the boat and along the sides for spraying water.

Draw a Yacht

Power yachts have motors instead of sails. They are known for being the most fancy personal boats. Often they not only have sleeping cabins, but also several other rooms. Some yachts are bigger than small houses.

1 Sketch a rectangle with angled sides for the **hull.**

2 Add two curved lines like a wave for the **spoiler.**

3 Draw a curved line from the front of the hull for the first level of cabins. Add another curved line on top of the one you just drew for the second level of cabins. Draw a rectangle with a curved top behind the spoiler.

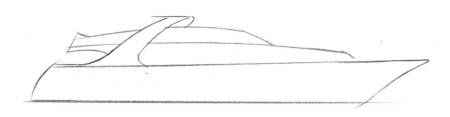

4 Draw three oval-shaped windows on the first level of cabins. Draw two rectangular windows on the second level.

5 Add details to the hull. Draw two **horizontal** lines across the side of the boat. Add a thin rectangle from the **stern.** Draw two small rectangles near the tip of the **bow** for portholes. Add curvy lines along the bottom of the boat for water.

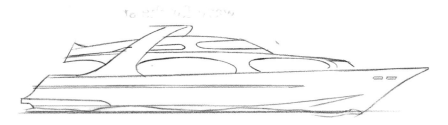

6 Darken the windows. Add two **vertical** lines for **antennae** on top of the spoiler. Draw a circle with an oval on top of it between the antennae. Darken all the lines of the drawing. Add **shading** around the boat for water.

Draw a Riverboat

The paddleboat steamer is powered by a steam engine that turns a big paddle wheel at the back of the boat. The wheel pushes the boat. These big riverboats are still popular with tourists along the Mississippi River.

1 **Sketch** a long, skinny rectangle with angled sides for the **hull.** Add a curved hump at one end for the **bow.**

2 Lightly sketch a large rectangle on top of the hull. Add another shorter rectangle and a square for the **decks.**

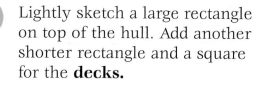

3 Draw an oval on the back of the boat for the paddle. Draw two long **vertical** lines for a flagpole on the front of the boat. Add two tall rectangles for smokestacks.

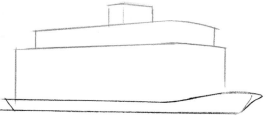

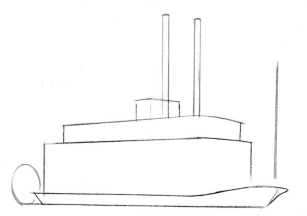

4 Draw a line **parallel** to the top of the hull for a railing. Add vertical lines connecting the top of the hull to the railing. Add railings with vertical lines to each of the other decks.

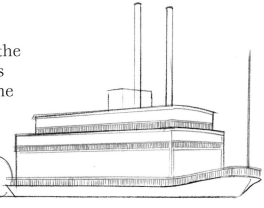

5 Add vertical lines for posts along the bottom deck. Draw a long line of small curves for arches along the top of the second and third decks. Draw posts on those decks. Draw an upside down 7 connecting the paddle to the back of the boat. Add lines like a bicycle wheel's spokes to the paddle.

6 Darken the lines in the drawing. Draw a big X with a line on top connecting the two smokestacks. Add **shading** to the smokestacks and along the tops of the decks. Add a few dark shapes for people. Draw a curvy rectangle for a flag. Add light, curvy lines for smoke. Lightly draw **horizontal** lines for water around the boat. Draw doors and stairs on the first deck.

Draw an America's Cup Yacht

The America's Cup is a trophy named after *America*, the yacht that first won it in 1851. The America's Cup race is usually held every three to four years. Teams from all over the world compete in this very famous sailboat race.

1 Draw a long, narrow oval with one pointed end and one straight end.

2 Draw two long **vertical** lines from the middle of the boat for the **mast.** Draw two **horizontal** lines from near the bottom of the mast for the **boom.**

3 Draw a curved line from the top of the mast to the boom for the **mainsail.**

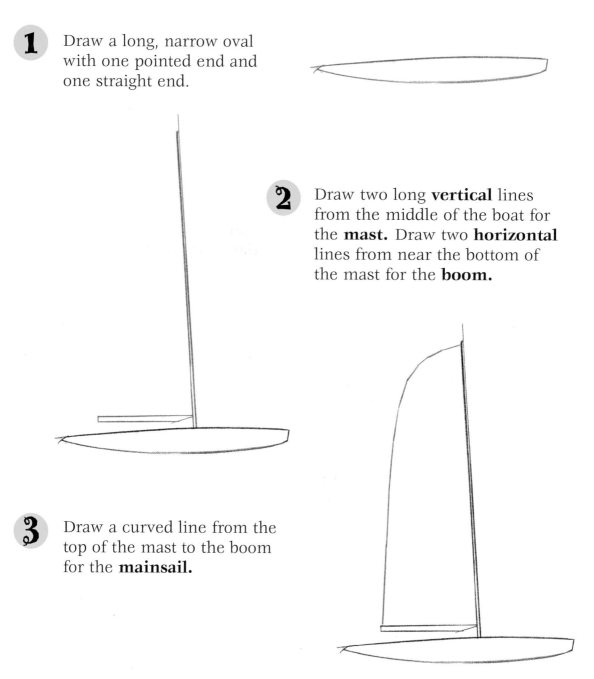

4 Add a curved triangle for the other sail.

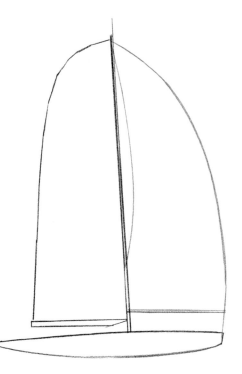

5 Add some horizontal supports to the mainsail and wires from the mast to the **hull.** Add five lines connecting the **jib** to the mast.

6 Darken the lines of the drawing. Add **shading** to the sails. Draw a square on the jib. Add the shapes of some people in the boat. Add shading and squiggly lines for the water. Draw art on the sails. Add the **horizon** behind the boat.

USA 12

Glossary

armed having weapons

antennae wires or structures that pick up and send out radio waves

bamboo plant that has a lightweight, hollow, wood-like stem

boom horizontal piece of wood or fiberglass that keeps the bottom of a sail in place

bow front of the boat

bowsprit piece that extends from the front of the ship, often for decoration

commercial artist person who designs and illustrates things for other people

deck floor of a boat

horizon line in the distance where the sky and land or water meet

hull part of the boat that sits in the water

jib the smaller sail on a two-sail sailboat

keel piece of wood or fiberglass that hangs down from the bottom of a boat and makes it stable in the water

mainsail the bigger sail on a two-sail sailboat

mast main pole to which the sails are attached

propeller wheel with blades that spin and push a boat through water

radar equipment that uses radio waves to find another object

rudder blade at the back of a boat that turns it

slats long, thin pieces of wood or other material

spoiler fin-shaped device attached to the back of a vehicle

stern back of a boat

Art Glossary

crosshatches lines that cross each other like a net

guideline
light line, used to shape a drawing, that is usually erased in the final drawing

horizontal
line that is level or flat

kneaded eraser
soft, squeezable eraser, used to soften dark pencil lines

parallel lines that lie next to one another but never touch

shade
make darker than the rest

sketch
draw quickly and roughly

vertical line that is straight up and down

More Books to Read

Books About Drawing

La Placa, Michael. *How to Draw Boats, Trains and Planes.* Mahwah, New Jersey: Troll Communications, 1997.

Norrington, Robert. *Sketching Harbors and Boats.* London: Cassell, 1999.

Books About Watercraft

Hill, Lee Sullivan. *Get Around on Water.* Minneapolis, Minnesota: Carolrhoda Books, 2000.

Oxlade, Chris. *Ships.* Hauppauge, New York: Barron's Education Series, 2001.

Index